B.C. One More Time

Johnny Hart

CORONET BOOKS
Hodder Fawcett, London

First published in Great Britain 1976
by Coronet Books

Second impression 1977
Third impression 1979

Printed and bound in Great Britain for
Hodder Fawcett Ltd, Mill Road, Dunton Green,
Sevenoaks, Kent (Editorial Office:
47 Bedford Square, London WC1 3DP), by
Hunt Barnard Printing Ltd, Aylesbury, Bucks.

ISBN 0 340 20653 5

BZZZZZZZZz

BAMP

hart

2

SPURT

I'M LEAVING YOU SHIRLEY! MY BELOVED MUSHROOM AWAITS ME.
SOB
LIFE IS A BITTER PILL, SHIRL!
hart

WHAT HAVE YOU GOT THERE?
IT'S A TURKEY CALL.
LET ME TRY THAT.
GOBBLE GOBBLE GOBBLE
DON'T SUCK, STUPID, ... BLOW!

WHERE'S DAD, MOM?
HE'S BRINGING HOME THE TREE.
DRAG DRAG DRAG DRAG DRAG
HERE HE COMES NOW.
ZOT
OH MY GOSH!, IT'S THE ANTEATER!
IT'S OK, MA, HE LEFT THE TREE!
hart

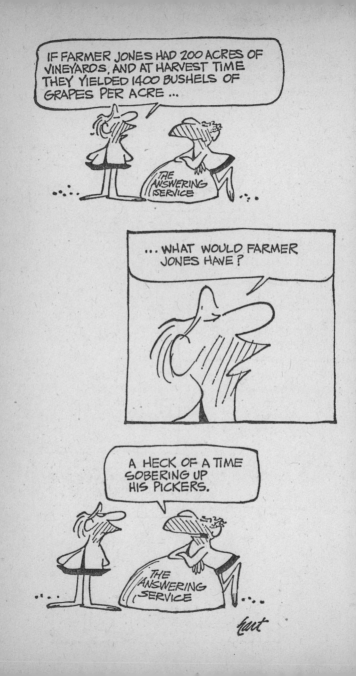

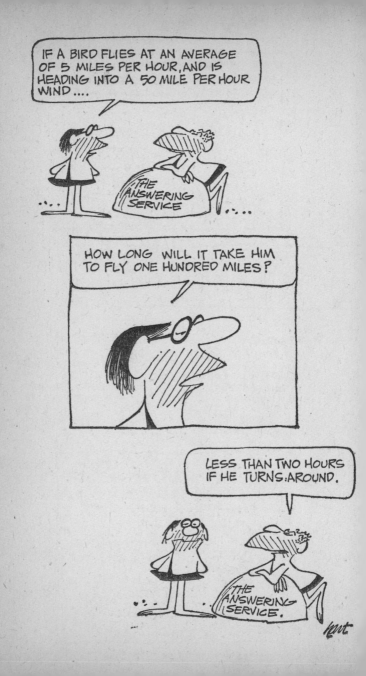

FARMER BROWN TAKES A COW TO MARKET AND TRADES HIM FOR A BUSHEL OF BEANS, THEN PLANTS THE BEANS, SELLS HIS CROP AND BUYS TWO COWS.

THE ANSWERING SERVICE

HOW LONG WILL FARMER BROWN HAVE TO WAIT TO BECOME A CATTLE BARON?

UNTIL HE WISES UP AND BUYS A BULL!

THE ANSWERING SERVICE

PING

MUNCH
MUNCH
MUNCH
MUNCH
MUNCH

MUNCH
MUNCH
MUNCH
MUNCH

THE POOR BEGGAR GOT THE ONE WITH THE GRISTLE.

LAP
LAP
LAP
LAP
LAP
LAP
LAP
LAP

POOF

SPRAAAACK

BLIPPITY BLOP
BLOPPITY BLIP
BLEEP CHUNK
RUKKA RUKKA
JIMP BLOP
KACHUNK
KACHUNK
ANTIQUES
HOW MUCH WILL YOU GIVE ME ON THIS WHEEL?
ANTIQUES
ABOUT ANOTHER MILE AND A HALF.
ANTIQUES

FLUMMFF

BLAAAAAA

THAT'S THE LAST TIME I BUY
A STEWARDESS 'CALL BUTTON'
FROM A CHEAP WHOLESALE HOUSE.

CORONET CARTOONS

JOHNNY HART

☐ 18820 0	B.C. on the Rocks	50p
☐ 19474 X	B.C. Right On	60p
☐ 19873 7	B.C. Cave In	60p
☐ 16477 8	Back to B.C.	50p
☐ 16881 1	What's New B.C.	50p
☐ 18780 8	B.C. Is Alive and Well	50p
☐ 16880 3	B.C. Big Wheel	50p
☐ 20762 0	B.C. It's a Funny World	60p
☐ 21248 9	B.C. Dip in Road	50p

JOHNNY HART & BRANT PARKER

☐ 20529 6	Long Live the King	60p
☐ 20776 0	Wizard Of Id Yield	50p
☐ 18604 6	There's a Fly in My Swill	50p
☐ 15818 2	The Wondrous Wizard of Id	50p
☐ 16899 4	Remember the Golden Rule	50p
☐ 16476 X	The Peasants are Revolting	50p

All these books are available at your local bookshop or newsagent, or can be ordered direct from the publisher. Just tick the titles you want and fill in the form below.

Prices subject to change without notice.

CORONET BOOKS, P.O. Box 11, Falmouth, Cornwall.

Please send cheque or postal order, and allow the following for postage and packing:

U.K. – One book 22p plus 10p per copy for each additional book ordered, up to a maximum of 82p.

B.F.P.O. and Eire – 22p for the first book plus 10p per copy for the next 6 books, thereafter 4p per book.

Other Overseas Customers – 30p for the first book and 10p per copy for each additional book.

Name ....

Address ....

....